WORDS OF PROMISE

A Creative Minds Biography

WORDS OF PROMISE

A Story about James Weldon Johnson

by Jodie Shull

Illustrations by Ken Stetz

M Millbrook Press/Minneapolis

For Tina   *—J.S.*

To Rebecca, for her inspiration, enthusiasm and assistance with research   *—K.S.*

Lyrics from "Lift Every Voice and Sing" (James Weldon Johnson, J. Rosamond Johnson) used by permission of EDWARD B. MARKS MUSIC COMPANY

Text from ALONG THIS WAY by James Weldon Johnson, copyright 1933 by James Weldon Johnson, renewed © 1961 by Grace Nail Johnson. Used by permission of Viking Penguin, a division of Penguin Putnam Inc.

Millbrook Press
A division of Lerner Publishing Group
241 First Avenue North
Minneapolis, MN 55401 U.S.A.

Website address: www.lernerbooks.com

Library of Congress Cataloging-in-Publication Data

Shull, Jodie A.
    Words of promise : a story about James Weldon Johnson / by Jodie Shull ; illustrations by Ken Stetz.
      p.   cm. — (Creative minds biography)
    Includes bibliographical references and index.
    ISBN-13: 978–1–57505–755–2 (lib. bdg. : alk. paper)
    ISBN-10: 1–57505–755–7 (lib. bdg. : alk. paper)
      1. Johnson, James Weldon, 1871–1938—Juvenile literature. 2. Authors, American—20th century—Biography—Juvenile literature. 3. Civil rights workers—United States—Biography—Juvenile literature. I. Stetz, Ken. II. Title. III. Series.
    PS3519.O2625Z87 2006
    818'.5209—dc22   2004029358

Manufactured in the United States of America
1 2 3 4 5 6 – JR – 11 10 09 08 07 06

Table of Contents

1

High Hopes

Five-year-old Jim poked his head out and looked down the slow-moving line of children ahead. Eager and nervous, he hoped it wouldn't take too long to reach the wide hotel porch. Hundreds of black school-children, dressed in their best clothes, were parading past Ulysses S. Grant. Grant was visiting Jim's home-town of Jacksonville, Florida, early in 1877.

Jim had heard Grant's famous name all of his young life. Ulysses S. Grant had been president of the United States when Jim was born. Before that, he was the general who won the Civil War. Jim knew, too, about the ferocious fighting of the Civil War, though he didn't yet know what the fighting was about. Most boys in town had collections of rusty buttons, belt buckles, and bayonets left behind by soldiers in the sandy fields of Jacksonville.

Now Jim was going to see the great general up close. Would he have the courage to carry out his secret plan? Jim climbed the wooden steps to the hotel porch, watching his shoes touch each stair. At last, Jim stood looking up at the bearded chin of General Grant. Alone, of all the children, Jim bravely put his hand forward. General Grant took Jim's hand in his and held it for a moment. Jim smiled with pride and happiness. He had reached out to touch a part of his country's history. He had connected with a larger world where he knew he belonged.

Jim's parents, Helen and James Johnson, had taught him to believe in life's good possibilities. They wanted him to live with courage and confidence. Although they were African American, they had never experienced slavery. Helen was born in the Bahamas, British islands off the American coast. James was born to a free black family in Richmond, Virginia. When he was old enough, he traveled to New York to find work. Helen was a student in New York and James was a headwaiter at a large hotel when they met.

In 1861, the American Civil War began. Southern and Northern states fought each other. Slavery was one of the main reasons for the war. Helen and her mother returned to the Bahamas.

They were afraid that if the South won the war, slavery would extend to all of the United States. James Johnson loved Helen and followed her family to the Bahamas. They got married in the town of Nassau in 1864.

After the war ended, slavery was made illegal. Helen and James returned to the United States. James chose the small town of Jacksonville, Florida, for their new home. American visitors to the Bahamas had told him that Jacksonville was a town with a great future in the tourist business and a welcoming place for black citizens.

James Weldon Johnson, or Jim, was born in Jacksonville on June 17, 1871. Two years later, John Rosamond Johnson was born. Jim and Rosamond were constant companions. Their father held the position of headwaiter at the elegant St. James Hotel. Their mother worked at the all-black Stanton School. She was the first female African American schoolteacher in the state of Florida.

By the time Jim met General Grant, his mother had taught him to read and write and play the piano. His father taught him to play the guitar. Surrounded by books at home, Jim became a boy who loved learning. He attended Stanton School, and his parents encouraged him to work hard at school. They also taught him to be considerate of other people and to help anyone who was less fortunate.

Growing up in Jacksonville in the 1870s, Jim didn't see much of the poverty and misfortune that many black children suffered in the southern United States. His happy and comfortable home was filled with the sound of his mother's beautiful voice, singing and reading aloud, and the smell of his grandmother's delicious crab stew and johnnycake.

Jim dreamed about his future. He was good at so many things, how could he ever decide what to be when he grew up? One summer he got a job delivering newspapers and began helping out in the newspaper office too. Writing news stories looked like a job he might like to try. He also thought he might want to be a drummer in a marching band, a driver of horses, a baseball player, a writer, a lawyer, a doctor, or the governor of Florida.

One thing Jim did know about his future, he would decide it for himself. Like his independent and capable parents, he would be a free citizen of a free country. When he was thirteen, Jim had a chance to see part of the new and larger world that waited for him. He discovered that he could feel at home not only on the country roads of Jacksonville, but also on the bustling streets of New York City.

In the summer of 1884, he boarded a ship with his Grandmother Mary. They traveled north to visit relatives in the New York borough of Brooklyn. Boroughs are sections of New York City that are made up of many neighborhoods. It was Jim's first visit to America's largest city, but he felt he belonged there. For as long as he could remember, his parents had talked about New York as home. Now, at last, he could see the magical city for himself.

Jim especially loved going into Manhattan, the busy center of New York City. Great-uncle William took Jim along on shopping trips to buy supplies for his business. They rode the ferry from Brooklyn, crossing over the churning water, where sailing ships from around the world moved toward the docks. Then Jim and Great-uncle William rode the horse-drawn street car through the crowded streets of Manhattan.

Jim had never seen so many people or such tall buildings. Enormous stores sold everything from buttons to billiard tables. Jim walked across the famous Brooklyn Bridge, finished just a year earlier. He rode the goat carts up and down the shady pathways of Central Park. He returned to Florida with great stories to tell his brother, Rosamond, and a heart filled with dreams for the future.

2

The Problem of Race

When Jim was fourteen, a black Cuban boy about his age came to live with the Johnsons. Ricardo Ponce's family wanted him to learn to speak English and become a dentist. He was like a brother to Jim and Rosamond. They helped Ricardo with his English, and he taught them Spanish. Three active and noisy boys kept things lively at the Johnson house.

In May of 1887, at age sixteen, Jim finished the eighth grade at Stanton School. The teachers advanced the students slowly because there was no hurry to graduate. For most students, no further education was available. The public high school in Jacksonville did not accept black students. Jim would have to leave home to finish high school and prepare for college.

That fall Jim was on his way to Atlanta, Georgia. Ricardo was going too. The boys would enroll in a high school there that prepared students to enter Atlanta University. Jim and his family had chosen Atlanta because it was the black college closest to Jacksonville.

When Jim and Ricardo boarded the overnight train for school, Jim wasn't sure whether to feel happy or sad. Going to Atlanta was an exciting adventure, but he would miss his family and friends very much. To cheer himself up, he thought about the fried chicken, oranges, and cake his mother had packed for the trip. He and Ricardo would eat them as soon as the train chugged out of the station.

The train's conductor appeared suddenly in the doorway of the first-class car. He hurried straight to Jim and said, "You had better get out of this car and into the one ahead." Jim was astonished and showed the conductor their first-class tickets. The conductor shook his head. "You'll be likely to have trouble if you try to stay in this car." The state of Florida had just passed a new law—separate train cars for blacks and whites.

Ricardo heard the conductor's words, but he didn't understand. *"Qué dice?"* (What's he saying?), he asked Jim. Jim told Ricardo in Spanish that the conductor wanted them to leave the first-class car because they were black.

The conductor looked puzzled. Because the boys spoke Spanish, he decided they must be foreigners and not black American citizens. He punched their tickets and moved on. Only black Americans had to obey the unfair laws of racial separation. The boys were shocked, scared, and angry. It was Jim's first face-to-face encounter with racial prejudice.

During Jim's growing-up years in Jacksonville, he never thought about being black. His family's race was never a problem or a worry for him. When he traveled to Atlanta, he left the sheltered world of his childhood. He learned what it meant to be black in America near the turn of the twentieth century.

By 1887 blacks throughout the South were losing the freedoms they had gained after the Civil War. The government program of Reconstruction, designed to repair the damage done by slavery and ensure the rights of African Americans, had ended. Southern states were passing laws of separation that kept blacks from having the rights of free American citizens. In Atlanta, Jim would find the problem of race always in the hearts and minds of his fellow students.

In the fall of 1890, Jim had graduated from the high school and began attending Atlanta University. His studies included history, literature, science, Latin, and Greek. He was a star player on the school's baseball team and a lead singer in the college choir. During the summer of 1891, after his freshman year at the university, Jim had a chance to gain a new kind of knowledge and experience. Atlanta University students were encouraged to teach summer school for poor black farm children in the backwoods of Georgia. Jim taught for two summers in the farm country of Henry County in a school without desks or books. He tried to help his students learn to read and write in the short time they had together. It was his first contact with southern black children who spent their days planting and harvesting cotton.

Jim discovered that life for these families wasn't much different from their grandparents' lives as slaves. Poverty and lack of education kept them working on rented farms. They grew cotton and other crops for large landowners and received a share of the harvest for their pay. They worked hard but never made enough money to buy land or send their children to school. Without education, they couldn't fight for a voice in government. White people who benefited from their hard work ignored or mistreated them.

Jim knew that life had to be made better for his students and their parents, but how could it be done? He considered all the problems that black people faced.

It seemed hopeless. But these country black people, his people, were not hopeless. Jim often heard them laughing and singing. He decided their laughter and song must come from great strength and courage.

Jim stayed with his students' families in their small, tumbledown cabins and shared their meals of greens and cornbread. He learned to respect and admire the hard-working black farm families. Teaching for a few months seemed like a small contribution, but it set Jim thinking about bigger ways he could help.

Jim graduated from Atlanta University in May of 1894 at the age of twenty-three. At the university, he had learned to be an excellent public speaker. He was chosen to give a graduation speech to his classmates. He was proud of himself for overcoming his childhood fear of speaking to a large group.

Now Jim had a decision to make. Should he apply for a scholarship to study medicine at Harvard University? Or should he return home to Jacksonville and take a job at Stanton School? The school he had graduated from seven years before needed a new principal. Jim had learned many things at Atlanta University. Most important of all, he said, the college had prepared him to be "a leader and helper to my race." Jim decided to return to Jacksonville and see what he could accomplish.

3

Lift Every Voice

As Stanton's new principal, Jim wanted to learn all he could about running a good school. Early that fall of 1894, he visited the all-white grammar school in Jacksonville. The principal of the white school was a friend and welcomed Jim's request for help. Jim wanted to see how things were done at the white school and make sure that Stanton School was keeping up.

Jim spent part of the morning talking to the principal and then asked if he could visit the classrooms. He wanted to see how teachers at the white school worked with their students. Were Stanton teachers working the same way? Jim went from room to room, introducing himself to the teachers and then sitting in class to observe for a while. Some of the white teachers welcomed him. Others were stiffly polite. The students stared at him with great curiosity.

Jim came away feeling good about his visit to the white school. He was shocked several days later when he was called to a meeting of the board of education. White parents had heard about his visit and complained to the board. As long as there had been public schools in Jacksonville, blacks and whites had been separated. White parents demanded to know why a black man was visiting their school.

It was hard for Jim to believe that the meeting was serious. He knew all the board of education members and thought they must be terribly embarrassed at having to respond to such a silly complaint. But the matter was serious. Luckily for Jim, the white principal who had encouraged his visit spoke to the board and ended the questioning. White parents were reassured that no one intended to violate the color barrier.

The Jacksonville of Jim's childhood, the friendly climate for blacks, was disappearing. White determination to keep the races separate was spreading throughout the South. As the 1890s passed, laws of racial separation multiplied in the southern states. The name Jim Crow, from a black character in a popular song, was used for these laws that segregated, or separated, whites and blacks. The laws required separate cars on trains, separate seats in public buildings, separate schools, and separate cemeteries.

Jim watched the increase in Jim Crow laws with growing concern. He could see it was going to be harder than ever to win fair treatment and equal opportunity for his people. After his first year as principal at Stanton, he asked his graduating eighth graders to come back in the fall. With the help of an assistant, he taught classes for ninth and tenth graders over the next two years. He hoped someday to offer a full high school program at Stanton. Creating a high school would be the first step toward making education for blacks equal to education for whites in Jacksonville.

Jim had a lot of energy, and he wanted to follow as many of his dreams as he could. He had come to believe in the power of words. During the spring of 1895, he decided to start a daily newspaper especially for the black community. With a friend's help and some borrowed money, he bought printing equipment and began publishing the *Daily American*. It was the first newspaper for blacks to be published every day.

The paper was very successful at first. In daily editorials, Jim wrote about his ideas for the progress of black citizens. His goal was to promote understanding between whites and blacks. He pointed out news of interest to blacks and spoke out against injustice. He also encouraged blacks to learn new skills and educate themselves for a better life.

Jim's newspaper business came to an end after only eight months. The cost of publishing a paper every day was too high. And it was hard to run a school and a newspaper at the same time. Jim was very disappointed. He decided to pursue another dream.

Jim had often thought about becoming a lawyer. But he couldn't afford to go north to a law school that would accept blacks. Instead, he got a part-time job in the law office of an experienced lawyer, Thomas Ledwith. He spent eighteen months reading law books and learning legal work with Ledwith's help. By the spring of 1898, Jim was ready to take an oral test to practice law in the state of Florida.

Jim stayed up very late studying the night before his test. When he arrived at the courthouse in the morning, he was glad to see his friend Thomas Ledwith there to encourage him. In fact, the courthouse was filled with people. No black person in Duval County had ever applied to be a lawyer in this way before. Jim didn't want to make himself nervous by looking at the large crowd.

For two hours, Jim answered questions about the law for a panel of three white lawyers and one white judge. Jim knew the reputations of all four men. Only one worried him. Three men were considered fair and just on the subject of race. The fourth man was known to be a racist. He made Jim's examination as difficult as he could. But Jim had studied well and knew the answers to all the questions. No one could deny that Jim was qualified. Finally, the white lawyer stormed out of the courtroom. He said he would not stay to see a black person take the oath to practice law.

After Jim passed his test to be a lawyer, he started a law practice. He spent his days at Stanton School and his evenings doing legal work. He also found time to write poetry. One day Rosamond read Jim's note-book of poems. Rosamond thought the poems would make good songs and wrote music for some of them. Rosamond was a master of musical notes. He could sing, play the piano beautifully, and compose music. He gave music lessons in the Johnson home. The two brothers discovered that they made an excellent song-writing team.

Early in 1900, Jim was asked to help plan a cele-bration in Jacksonville for the birthday of Abraham

Lincoln, the American president who had freed the slaves during the Civil War. Jim offered to give a speech, but he wanted to do something more. He asked Rosamond to help him write a song for the celebration.

Jim sat down and began to write. He thought of a first line for his song—"Lift every voice and sing." He wanted to give the singers and the listeners a feeling of hope and celebration. Though Lincoln had ended slavery, the effort to win freedom and equality for black people had made only a little progress by 1900. Jim wanted to encourage blacks to be proud of their heritage and to keep working for justice. He wanted whites to listen to the call for fairness and friendship.

Jim wrote the first verse of his song and gave it to Rosamond. Rosamond sat at the piano picking out a tune. Jim walked back and forth on the front porch planning more lines for the song in his head. Tears ran down his cheeks as he paced. The thoughts behind the song stirred his deepest emotions. He loved putting his thoughts and feelings into words. Words had power and promise.

Jim and his brother had decided that a chorus of five hundred schoolchildren would sing "Lift Every Voice and Sing" at the celebration on February 12.

The students learned the song and performed it beautifully:

> Lift every voice and sing
> Till earth and heaven ring,
> Ring with the harmonies of Liberty.

When the chorus finished singing, the large audience of Jacksonville citizens burst into applause.

After the celebration, Jim and Rosamond didn't think about the song again until many years later. They discovered that their students had carried the song to schools and churches throughout the South. People loved the song for its message of hope and inspiration. The brothers were amazed and thrilled to hear their celebration hymn being called the Negro National Anthem. "We wrote better than we knew," Jim said.

4

Brothers on Broadway

One afternoon in May of 1901, Jim and Rosamond were riding their bicycles home from a choir rehearsal. The brothers saw smoke rising from the western edge of the city. As they raced toward home, they met people running away from a huge fire. The fire was only two blocks from Stanton School. Jim and Rosamond hurried to the school and gathered up all the important papers they could carry. They headed home and were relieved to find that the Johnson house was safe. By nighttime, more than twenty friends had come to the house looking for shelter. All had lost their homes.

In the terrible fire, two-thirds of the city of Jacksonville burned to the ground, including Stanton School. Help arrived from other cities. State soldiers took charge of the ruined town. These men from the backwoods counties of Florida were strangers to Jacksonville. They spoke rudely to the black citizens and treated them with suspicion and disrespect.

Jim had a frightening encounter with some soldiers one day in the city park. A friend of Jim's who worked as a reporter for a northern black newspaper came to Jacksonville to write about the fire. She and Jim talked about the disaster as they walked through a city park. Suddenly, they found themselves surrounded by soldiers with guns. The soldiers thought Jim's light-skinned friend was white. To the soldiers, Jim was not the respected principal of Stanton School. He was a strange black man who seemed to be socializing with a white woman.

Jim knew what to do. He showed no anger or fear. He looked for the soldier in charge and asked to be taken to military headquarters. Safely away from the excitable soldiers and their weapons, Jim explained the situation to the commander and received an apology.

Rosamond was very upset when Jim told him what had happened. Jim had to agree. No matter what job he held or what he had accomplished, he was still a black man in a southern town. A small misunderstanding could cost him his freedom or even his life.

Jim and Rosamond decided it would be safest to leave Jacksonville for the summer. They headed for New York City. Rosamond had many friends in the music business there.

Jim and Rosamond made a home for themselves at the Marshall Hotel in the New York neighborhood of Harlem. Jim remembered Harlem from his childhood visits as an empty corner of northern Manhattan with more goats than people. Now houses lined the streets, and a small black community was growing. The Marshall Hotel was a three-story brownstone house with a restaurant on the bottom floor. Jim and Rosamond rented a room upstairs, brought in a piano, and set up a songwriting workshop.

Even in big northern cities like New York, many restaurants and hotels refused to serve black customers. The Marshall Hotel in Harlem became a friendly gathering place for black artists, writers, and musicians. On Sundays a musical show followed dinner. The good food and good company made Jim and Rosamond feel at home.

That summer Jim and Rosamond lived in the heart of America's songwriting capital. Musical shows that traveled all over the country were written and performed first in the Broadway theater district of New York. The brothers wrote songs for famous singers and producers who needed music for new shows.

Jim and Rosamond formed a partnership with their friend, singer and dancer Bob Cole. The team of Cole and the Johnson Brothers became well known on Broadway. Jim wrote the words for their songs. Rosamond and Bob wrote and performed the music. They signed a contract with a music publisher in 1901 and sold more than a dozen songs. Recorded music was rare and expensive at that time. Like most popular music of the day, the Johnsons' songs were published as sheet music. People bought copies of the songs they liked to play on their pianos at home.

Jim loved being part of New York's black music community. He thought about his future. When Stanton School was rebuilt and opened again, did he want to return to his job as principal? Compared to his job at Stanton, songwriting didn't seem like a real occupation. But Jim loved to create. His songs, like his poems, came from his heart. Using his imagination made him happy. He decided to stay in New York with Rosamond and Bob.

By summer of 1902, the songs of Cole and the Johnson Brothers were selling very well. The trio was making enough money to rent the entire second floor of the Marshall Hotel. They had plenty of work creating songs for the biggest musical shows on Broadway.

That summer they wrote their most successful number, a love song called "Under the Bamboo Tree."

Their rooms at the Marshall Hotel served as a home, a music studio, and a meeting place for black entertainers and friends. Jim was well liked by the many black families he met in New York. They often invited him to their homes for dinners and parties. He especially enjoyed visiting his friend Jack Nail in Brooklyn. Jack's younger sister Grace became a special friend of Jim's. Grace shared Jim's love of books, music, and plays.

In the next year, Rosamond and Bob developed a song and dance act. Rosamond played the piano and sang. Bob sang and danced. Jim was a good singer and guitar player, but he preferred writing to being on stage. He stayed in New York when Rosamond and Bob traveled to theater jobs out of town.

Jim decided to use his spare time in New York to continue his education. He wanted to learn all he could about musical theater. He enrolled at Columbia University to take classes in drama and literature. On Saturday nights, he attended bargain shows at New York theaters and went to all the operas at the Metropolitan Opera House.

Jim's professor at Columbia University, Brander Matthews, had heard the songs of Cole and the

Johnson Brothers and liked them. He welcomed Jim to his classes and often talked to him about theater and creative writing. Jim began writing a book. Jim's book was a fictional story about being black in America.

Jim called his book *The Autobiography of an Ex-Colored Man.* It is the imaginary life story of a man whose heritage is mixed black and white. His light skin allows him to pass over the color line and blend in with white society. He is able to experience life in America sometimes as a black person and sometimes as a white one. Jim wanted this invented life story to help American whites understand what it felt like to be black, always treated as different and inferior. Because of his sadness and fear, the hero of Jim's story decides to spend his life as a white man. Jim's "ex-colored man" feels ashamed of his choice. He wishes he had the courage to live as a black man and help in the fight for a better life. Jim would continue working on his novel for several years.

5

Travels

In the summer of 1905, Rosamond and Bob were offered a chance to perform at the Palace Theater in London. They invited Jim to come along. A trip to Europe was too exciting for Jim to pass up. What would it feel like to be a black American in a foreign country? Jim discovered that it felt wonderful. Racial prejudice didn't seem to exist in Europe. For the first time since his childhood, Jim felt the freedom of being just a person and not a black person in a white world.

The trio visited the cities of Paris, Brussels, and Amsterdam before traveling to London. To their amazement, they found the city of London filled with billboards advertising "Cole and Johnson, the Great American Musicians." Bob, Rosamond, and Jim were very nervous before the first show. They hoped they could live up to London's high expectations.

Thundering applause on opening night told them the show was a great success.

The trip to Europe was a wonderful adventure. More than anything, Jim enjoyed meeting the people in foreign cities. He liked exploring new places and seeing lives completely different from his own. The journey was a success in every way except one. The cost of the trip was much higher than they expected. Bob Cole and the Johnsons arrived back in America with only a little change in their pockets.

Jim began to worry that he still hadn't found the real work he was meant to do in the world. He was less interested now in writing popular songs. Bob and Rosamond decided to travel the country full-time with their own theater group. That life was not for Jim.

A friend suggested that Jim apply for government work. Under President Theodore Roosevelt, some United States foreign service jobs were available for blacks. His college education, language skills, and calm, polite manner made Jim a good candidate. He took an examination in Washington, D.C. In a few months, Jim had a new job.

Because he spoke Spanish, Jim was assigned to a post in South America. He would be America's representative in Puerto Cabello, Venezuela. Jim was excited to be setting off for a new world, but he was also sorry to leave New York. He called the great city his "fairy godmother" because so many good things had happened to him there. In the summer of 1906, at the age of thirty-five, Jim sailed south to the Caribbean Sea.

Puerto Cabello was a small seaport city where ships from many countries docked to load and unload cargo. Jim liked the look of his new home with its distant mountains, lush tropical landscape, and red-roofed, Spanish-style buildings. The circular harbor was the heart of a sunken volcano filled with seawater.

In his office near the wharf, Jim quickly learned his new job. He checked the papers of American ships arriving at the harbor. He wrote reports about business activities and political events in Venezuela.

Jim enjoyed getting to know the residents of Puerto Cabello. They accepted him as a respected member of the community. As in Europe, Jim didn't have to worry about the problem of race. His quiet life in Puerto Cabello gave him plenty of time for reading and writing. He wrote poetry and sent his poems to American magazines. Several were published while he lived in South America. He also finished work on his novel.

After three years in Puerto Cabello, Jim was promoted to a new position in Corinto, Nicaragua. Corinto, a tiny village on the Pacific coast of Central America, was a very busy port for trading and military ships. The harbor was beautiful, with a skyline of five volcanoes. But Jim's heart sank when he saw the town, which was only a cluster of wooden buildings carved out of the jungle. The streets were unpaved, and there was no electricity.

Jim's new job in Corinto was a difficult one. Heavy traffic of ships and people passed through the busy port. Jim was responsible for helping American citizens in need and keeping an eye on the unstable government of Nicaragua. Military generals ruled the country, one often fighting with another for power. Jim developed new skills in peacemaking.

In Corinto, Jim had no time for reading and writing, but he did make one important decision about his life. He took time off to go to New York at the end of 1909. On February 10, 1910, when he was thirty-eight years old, Jim got married. His bride was his old friend, Grace Nail. She was a beautiful, well-educated woman from a wealthy black family. Jim had loved Grace since he first met her.

Grace had spent all of her life in New York City. Jim was worried about bringing her to live in Corinto.

Although she was shocked at first, Grace was brave about the hardships of life in the small village. She quickly learned Spanish and even got used to the frequent earthquakes. Jim realized how lonely he had been and how happy he was to have Grace beside him.

In the summer of 1912, Jim received a message. His father had died. When he got the news, Jim went to his bedroom and cried. He thought about the happy childhood his father had given him. He had good memories of his father teaching him to swim, fly a kite, and play the guitar. He was very grateful for their time together.

Jim decided that life in Corinto was too hard and lonely for Grace. He wasn't able to get a transfer to another post so he resigned from his government job in the fall of 1913. For a year, Jim and Grace lived with Jim's mother in Jacksonville. Jim wasn't sure what to do next. His mother hoped he would stay in Jacksonville and practice law. But conditions for black people in the South were not improving. Jim noticed how difficult it was for Grace to be comfortable in a state where Jim Crow laws made her a second-class citizen. Jim and Grace decided to return to New York. They would later bring Jim's mother to New York too.

Jim found an apartment for them near Grace's parents in Harlem. He wanted to try making a living as a writer. Jim knew he could write well. He had a special talent for communicating so that people would listen, even if they didn't agree. He had written a poem for the fiftieth anniversary of the Emancipation Proclamation, the Civil War document that ended slavery in the rebel states. The poem appeared in the *New York Times,* a widely read and influential newspaper. Both blacks and whites praised the poem. It contained inspiring words for people of both races.

Within a year, Jim found a job that was perfect for him. He was hired as an editorial writer for the *New York Age,* an important black newspaper. In his weekly column, he continued the work he had started almost twenty years earlier with his own newspaper in Jacksonville. He became a voice for the rights of black citizens.

6

A Long, Hard Fight

Jim's weekly words for the *New York Age* reached a wide audience. At age forty-five, his reputation as a spokesperson for equality spread across the country. In his writing, he urged white Americans to support justice for all. He encouraged black Americans to keep learning, stand up for their rights, and be proud of their heritage.

In the fall of 1916, Jim received a very important letter. The National Association for the Advancement of Colored People wanted him to work for them. Jim liked the work of the NAACP. Their goal was to secure civil rights, the basic rights of citizenship, for all Americans. Jim agreed with their methods of using public opinion and political pressure to fight for racial equality. The NAACP was a new organization. They needed a person like Jim to help them grow.

Jim felt honored and grateful for the job offer. All the events of his life had prepared him for this important work. As a teacher and principal, a lawyer, an entertainer, a diplomat, and a writer, he had learned the skills of talking to people and persuading them. He would need all his knowledge and experience now. Jim was eager to bring more people into the struggle for justice and a better society.

Jim's job as membership recruiter was to convince black Americans to join the NAACP, especially in the South where most blacks still lived. Jim knew the NAACP also needed the support of as many white Americans as possible. He began his travels early in 1917, holding large meetings in fifteen cities to gather new members. He contacted black churches, schools, and social clubs and asked them to arrange for him to speak. Often Jim arrived to find a large meeting hall overflowing with people waiting to hear his message. Jim told the people that America could not call itself a free country until every citizen had freedom and equal opportunity. Every time black citizens were denied the right to vote, to be educated, or to live and work where they chose, America suffered.

Everywhere he traveled, Jim set up new branches of the NAACP and signed up hundreds of new members. Jim loved the work even though it was hard and exhausting. At last he could use all of his talents for a cause he believed in. As a powerful public speaker, he was able to capture people's attention and touch their emotions. His friendly and polite manner helped him handle difficult and sometimes dangerous situations. He could inspire people and get them to work together. He kept reports about the NAACP's work flowing to newspapers and magazines.

In April of 1917, the United States entered World War I. Hundreds of thousands of black Americans volunteered to serve their country in the military. Tens of thousands more left their southern homes to take jobs in the industrial cities of the North. Racial prejudice followed them. As blacks began competing with whites for jobs, housing, and access to education, more problems developed between the races.

The NAACP needed Jim's help with these problems, too. He began to investigate incidents in which black citizens were attacked by angry white mobs. In the summer of 1917, Jim investigated a riot in East St. Louis, Illinois. A fight between black and white neighbors grew into a battle that swept the city. A black neighborhood was burned, leaving six thousand homeless. Hundreds of blacks were killed, including many children. Witnesses saw black women and children shot and thrown into the flames.

Although blacks were the victims of the riot, local law officials blamed members of the black community for the trouble. On behalf of the NAACP, Jim arranged for lawyers to help blacks who faced charges. He provided money for those who had lost their homes. Jim reported the facts and made sure America learned the truth about what happened in East St. Louis.

Back in New York, Jim suggested that the NAACP organize a silent parade to protest the race riot. On Saturday, July 28, ten thousand blacks of all ages marched down Fifth Avenue to the sound of muffled drums. Children in white clothing led the parade. Women in white followed, and men in black clothing brought up the rear. American flags waved from the tall buildings on Fifth Avenue. The marchers carried protest signs. One of them read, "Treat Us So That We May Love Our Country."

In December of 1918, Jim's mother became very sick. Jim spent every hour that he could by her bedside. She wanted to get well in time to hear Jim speak at Carnegie Hall, the famous New York auditorium.

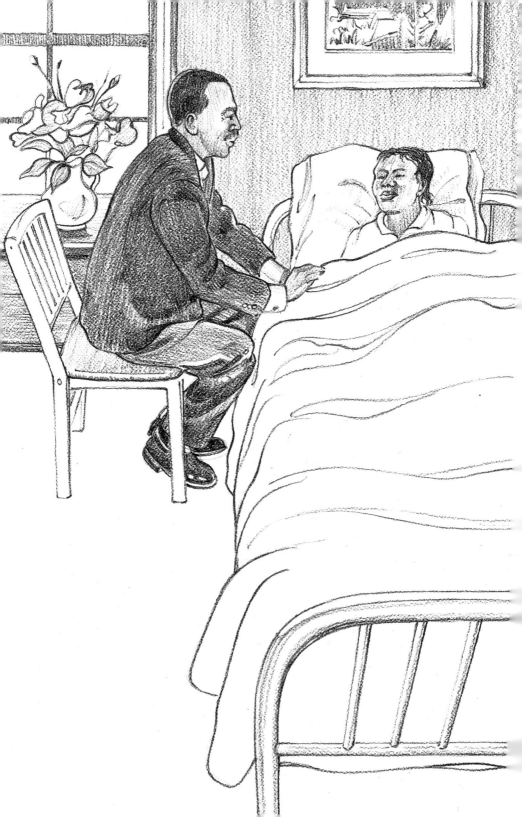

When the night of Jim's speech arrived, his mother was near death, but she insisted that Jim keep his appointment, even though she could not attend. Jim made what he felt was the best speech of his career, pleading for fair treatment of black soldiers returning from the war. After the speech, Jim returned to his mother's side. She died the next morning. Jim called the loss of his mother his life's greatest sorrow. She had been his first and best teacher. Her faith in him gave him the inner strength he needed to help others.

After three years of hard work, Jim had built a strong network of NAACP branches across the country. The number of members had grown to over 100,000. With a large membership, the NAACP could offer black Americans real help in the fight against injustice. In 1920 Jim became the first black chief executive, or leader, of the NAACP. The association had been founded by a group of white Americans who believed in racial equality. In Jim, they found a powerful black leader who could speak for the association to both blacks and whites. Jim was wise, kind, and reasonable. He could bring opposing groups together and work for the good of all.

Jim made his first goal as chief executive to fight for a national law against lynching. Lynching was the worst kind of violence being done to individual black

Americans. In a lynching, someone was accused of a crime and murdered without a trial. More than anything Jim wanted to stop these murders by white mobs.

Jim traveled to Washington, D.C., to ask the federal government for an anti-lynching law. For years, many states had allowed these murders to go unpunished because the victims were black and the murderers were white. Jim hoped a national law would force the states to prevent lynching and punish those who were guilty.

Jim planned a fight using public opinion and factual information. He felt that once the American people knew the truth about these crimes, justice would be done. For nearly two years, Jim spent most of his time in Washington. He visited lawmakers and talked about the importance of an anti-lynching law. It was hard, discouraging work. "Sometimes my heart was as sore and weary as my feet," he said.

The national law Jim worked for was never passed. But the fight against lynching did save many lives. The information provided to Congress and the public turned attention to the crime in a new way. The number of lynchings dropped by half in the ten years Jim served as chief executive of the NAACP.

7

Powerful Words

Jim continued his hard work for the NAACP through the 1920s. He and Grace lived in Harlem, and Jim took the subway each day to NAACP headquarters in downtown Manhattan. There he guided the work of members across the country. He wrote articles and letters and gave speeches whenever he could. He spread the news about the campaign for racial justice.

Jim believed the fight against prejudice required a change in thinking for both black and white Americans. Whites needed to respect blacks. But blacks also needed to respect themselves. Jim knew his ability to withstand prejudice came from self-respect. He worked hard to improve himself, to go where he wanted to go, and be what he wanted to be. He never let prejudice make him feel bad inside or doubt his ability. He wanted to help all black people build their pride.

Jim started to tell the world about the creative work of blacks. In 1922 he collected a book of poems by black writers and wrote a history of black poetry from colonial times to the 1920s. *The Book of American Negro Poetry* was the first collection ever made of the work of black poets.

In 1925 Jim and his brother, Rosamond, put together a book of songs from the folk music of black America. Rosamond lived in Harlem, too, and still worked in the music business. The brothers collected sixty-one spirituals, traditional religious folk songs. Spiritual singing had begun in the days of slavery. Later, the spirituals were sung in black churches across America. Rosamond arranged the songs for *The Book of American Negro Spirituals*. Jim's introduction explained the history of the songs and their importance in black culture. People loved the book so much that the brothers published a second collection of spirituals in 1926.

The book of spirituals made Jim remember another writing project he had dreamed of for years. On Thanksgiving Day, 1926, Jim sat down at his grandmother's old mahogany table and closed his eyes. When he was very young, his grandmother had taken him to a black southern church every Sunday. He remembered the preacher's voice rising and falling like music, delivering a sermon about love and justice. Now Jim wrote his own sermon in poetry. He called it "Go Down Death." It was a sermon of comfort for people who had lost a loved one.

Jim spent the Christmas holidays writing more of these sermons in poetry. They were published as a book in 1927. He wanted a musical title for his book. He called it *God's Trombones: Seven Negro Sermons in Verse*. In the book, he described the tradition of the black southern preacher. The preacher was an artist with words and one of the first voices of hope for black slaves in America. *God's Trombones* was part of Jim's work to help whites understand black culture and to give blacks pride in their heritage.

Jim saw good things happening in Harlem during the 1920s. The gathering of black musicians, writers, and artists that started in the early years of the century continued to grow. Jim was happy to find himself in the center of a great flowering of black art, music,

and literature. People later called these creative times the Harlem Renaissance. Jim made his own contributions to black literature by publishing his poetry and publishing a new edition of his novel in 1927. He also helped many other black writers publish their work and reach readers across the country.

After thirteen years with the NAACP, Jim was exhausted. His doctor warned him to slow down. Although Jim loved his busy life, in 1929 he decided to take a rest. He took a year off and wrote a history of blacks in New York called *Black Manhattan.* At the end of his time off, Jim decided to resign from the NAACP. He would leave the active work for younger people to carry on.

Jim was almost sixty years old when he retired from the NAACP. He felt comfortable moving into a less stressful life. He accepted a teaching job at Fisk University, a black college in Nashville, Tennessee. In his new position, Jim taught literature and creative writing from January to June. Jim's job gave him the free time he longed for. He spent his summers and falls writing and speaking about black culture and racial equality.

Jim wrote the story of his life and published it in 1933. *Along This Way* was the first published autobiography of a black man who had lived from the end of Reconstruction in the South through the exciting years of the Harlem Renaissance. Both whites and blacks admired Jim's book. He achieved what he hoped for. He brought readers together in a place beyond the problem of race. From his happy childhood through his many exciting careers, Jim's story could be enjoyed by all. "Life has been a stirring enterprise with me," he wrote. Readers could tell that Jim loved his life. He dedicated *Along This Way* to his wife, Grace.

Jim kept in contact with the NAACP and was often called on for advice. He was in great demand as a speaker and made as many speaking tours as his energy allowed. Shortly after he left his job with the NAACP, America entered the Great Depression. These years of unemployment and business failure destroyed the economic hopes of blacks and whites alike. Jim used his speaker's pay to help friends and relatives through the tough years of the 1930s.

In 1934 Jim outlined his hopes for the future in his book *Negro Americans, What Now?* He urged blacks to work together through organizations like the NAACP for equal rights and equal opportunity. He asked black Americans to look at their history with pride and their future with hope. He said he would never permit prejudice to damage his self-respect. He believed the problem of racial prejudice would be solved by blacks and whites working together. "If the Negro is made to fail," he wrote, "America fails with him."

Jim celebrated his sixty-seventh birthday in 1938 in New York, the city he loved. He and Grace then traveled north to visit some friends in Maine. While driving home on June 26, their car was struck by a train in a blinding rainstorm. Jim was killed, and Grace was badly injured.

The memorial service held for Jim at the Salem Methodist Church was one of the biggest in the history of Harlem. About 2,500 people, white and black, filled the church to honor James Weldon Johnson. He had spent his life keeping the promise of equality alive. Across America people continue to sing his freedom song, "Lift Every Voice and Sing."

Facing the rising sun of our new day begun,
Let us march on till victory is won.

Books by James Weldon Johnson

Along This Way: The Autobiography of James Weldon Johnson. New York: Viking Press, 1933.

The Autobiography of an Ex-Colored Man. Boston: Sherman, French & Co., 1912.

Black Manhattan. New York: Alfred A. Knopf, 1930.

The Book of American Negro Poetry. Edited by James Weldon Johnson. New York: Harcourt Brace and World, 1922.

The Book of American Negro Spirituals. Edited by James Weldon Johnson and J. Rosamond Johnson. New York: Viking Press, 1925.

God's Trombones: Seven Negro Sermons in Verse. New York: Viking Press, 1927.

Negro Americans, What Now? New York: Viking Press, 1934.

Bibliography

Bond, Julian, and Sondra Kathryn Wilson, eds. *Lift Every Voice and Sing: A Celebration of the Negro National Anthem, 100 years, 100 Voices.* New York: Random House, 2000.

Fairclough, Adam. *Better Day Coming: Blacks and Equality 1890–2000.* New York: Viking, 2001.

Fleming, Robert E. *James Weldon Johnson.* Boston: Twayne Publishers, 1987.

Johnson, James Weldon. *Along This Way: The Autobiography of James Weldon Johnson.* New York: Viking Press, 1933.

Johnson, James Weldon. *God's Trombones: Seven Negro Sermons in Verse.* Produced by Sondra Kathryn Wilson. St. Paul, MN: Penguin Highbridge, 1993. Audio cassette.

Levy, Eugene. *James Weldon Johnson: Black Leader, Black Voice.* Chicago: University of Chicago Press, 1973.

Lewis, David Levering. *When Harlem Was in Vogue.* New York: Oxford University Press, 1981.

Websites

The Academy of American Poets
http://www.poets.org/poets/

James Weldon Johnson, 1871–1938. Thomas Cooper Library at the University of South Carolina
http://www.sc.edu/library/spcoll/amlit/johnson/johnson.html

James Weldon Johnson
http://www.nku.edu/~diesmanj/johnson.html

Modern American Poetry: James Weldon Johnson
http://www.english.uiuc.edu/maps/poets/g_l/johnson/johnson.htm

Index

About the Author

Jodie Shull is a former elementary school librarian and English as a Second Language teacher. She worked for a historic small town newspaper in western Nevada while her children were young. Now she lives within walking distance of the ocean in Carlsbad, California.

About the Illustrator

Ken Stetz has illustrated for children and young adult readers since the early 1990s. His work appears on the pages of *Highlights for Children* and *Cricket* magazines. He has created illustrations for many published books including the fully illustrated children's book *Christmas Tails*. Ken lives in New Jersey with his wife, Diane, and their two children.